Raintree • Chicago, Illinois

BEING MAD, BEING GLAD

by Roger Day

Illustrated by Deborah Allwright

© 2005 Raintree
Published by Raintree, a division of Reed Elsevier Inc.
Chicago, Illinois

Customer Service 888-363-4266

Visit our website at www.raintreelibrary.com

Illustrated by Deborah Allwright
Packaged by Ticktock Media Ltd.
Designed by Robert Walster, BigBlu Design
Printed and bound in China, by South China Printing

09 08 07 06 05
10 9 8 7 6 5 4 3 2 1

Library of Congress Cataloging-in-Publication Data
Day, Roger, 1946-
  Being mad, being glad / Roger Day.
     p. cm. -- (Kids' guides)
  Includes bibliographical references and index.
  Contents: Anger and fear -- Jealousy and joy -- Sadness and loneliness -- Talking it through -- What would you do?
  ISBN 1-4109-0570-5 (lib. bdg.)
  1. Child psychology--Juvenile literature. 2. Emotions in children--Juvenile literature. [1. Emotions.] I. Title. II. Series: Kids' guides (Chicago, Ill.)
  HQ772.5.D38 2005
  155.4'124--dc22

                              2003021984

Some words are shown in bold, **like this.** You can find out what they mean by looking in the glossary.

CONTENTS

INTRODUCTION

This is a book about feelings. Our feelings are important. There are two kinds: **real feelings** and **cover-up feelings.**

When I get angry, I want to run away or start crying.

The four real feelings are anger, fear, joy, and sadness. We get sad about **painful loss.** We get angry to protect ourselves from harm or sort out problems. We feel fear about things that might happen in the future. We feel joyful when we are relaxed and ready for what tomorrow might bring.

I'm so happy I want to burst!

We have cover-up feelings, such as **jealousy** and **loneliness,** so we do not have to show or deal with how we really feel. Cover-up feelings leave us feeling bad or **confused.**

All my friends have better toys. I wish I had new toys like theirs.

When I'm scared, my heart starts pounding.

A mom sounds angry when her child runs into the road. But she is probably feeling scared. A friend may be mean to you, but they might be feeling sad about something that happened at home.

It is best to show your real feelings so people can understand you and help you. If you can't, you should talk to someone. This book will show you how.

Let's Talk About...
ANGER AND FEAR

I want to hit something!

Anger lets out some **energy** and can help you sort out your problems or protect you from harm. You get angry when someone is hurting you or if something doesn't seem right or fair. When you are angry you can also get pouty or upset. You may want to break things or hit people.

WHY DO I FEEL LIKE THIS?
Anger and fear are normal **emotions** and it is good to talk about them. It is not good to hurt people or break things.

Your anger affects other people, so find a safe way to let it out:

- Write it down or draw it.
- Count to ten.
- Shout loudly.
- Kick a ball or run fast.
- Punch a pillow.
- Tear up unwanted paper.

BUT WHY ME?

You aren't the only one. Many people do not show their feelings. But they probably feel the same way you do.

I'm scared!

People get afraid about the future, of **new situations,** or of bad things happening to their family. Fear can give you weak legs, an upset stomach, or a racing heart.

I'm afraid of the dark.

Fear is a good thing. It stops you from running into the road or walking off with a stranger. But some fears aren't helpful. You may be afraid of things that can't hurt you, such as thunder or scary movies.

LOOK AT IT ANOTHER WAY

Anger and fear are normal emotions. But sometimes when you have them, people find you hard to deal with. If you have these feelings a lot, adults may worry about you. Try to find good ways to let out your feelings.

If you feel scared, you can:

- Watch something funny on TV.
- Ask a grown-up to say everything is okay.
- Turn scary change into an exciting adventure.

Let's Talk About...
JEALOUSY AND JOY

He gets everything he wants.

Jealousy is wanting to be like someone else. **Envy** is wanting things others have. These are **cover-up feelings** for anger. You may be jealous when someone else gets all the attention or be envious of a friend's toys. Jealous or envious people become unfriendly or want to ruin things.

I'm so jealous of my sister. Why didn't I get a party?

Here are some ways out of jealousy and envy:

● Let out anger in a safe way.

● Remember life isn't always fair.

● Enjoy your own things.

● Think about good things people have said about you.

BUT WHY ME?

Most people get jealous at one time or another. Find ways of turning jealousy into joy. Be grateful for your own things. Some people have less than you do.

Mom's got a great new boyfriend. He's taking us to Disneyland!

Joy is when you are happy with life and with what you have. It is one of the nicest feelings.

When you are joyful you may feel like dancing or shouting with excitement. Some people feel like singing when they are happy. There are several things you can do:

- Laugh, sing, dance, and enjoy it.
- Celebrate the way you are feeling right now.
- Remember this feeling next time you have unhappy feelings.

WHY DO I FEEL LIKE THIS?

If you are feeling jealous, you might not think of anything else. This is not a good feeling. Joy is being happy, excited, and pleased, all at the same time.

LOOK AT IT ANOTHER WAY

When you are happy, other people may try to ruin your good feeling because they feel jealous. It may be better to save your excitement for when you are not with them.

Let's Talk About...

SADNESS AND LONELINESS

People feel sad about losing something they can never get back. Someone may have died. You may have moved or your family may have broken up. Sadness is a strong feeling. It is a healthy feeling even though it isn't nice. It is our way of saying good-bye. You may have an empty feeling or pain inside.

It helps to:

- Cry. You won't need to cry forever.
- Talk to someone about how you feel.
- Draw or write about your feelings.

> Sometimes I'm sad. I get an empty feeling in my chest.

WHY DO I FEEL LIKE THIS?

Sadness is a feeling of loss. You cry until you are able to let go. Sometimes this takes a long time. Loneliness is usually sadness or fear in disguise.

BUT WHY ME?

Everyone feels sad when they lose someone or something. You feel lonely when you think no one cares about you.

Everyone wants to be alone sometimes. **Loneliness** is different. Lonely people feel like they are on their own and feel sorry for themselves. They may want to hide away because they are sad. They may feel lonely when no one is near them.

I'm lonely because I don't have any brothers and sisters to play with.

Let's swap! Sometimes I'd love to get away from my sisters and be on my own.

If you feel lonely:

● Talk to someone about the way you feel.
● Tell people you want to be their friend.
● Discover ways to cheer yourself up.
● Find things to laugh and get excited about.

LOOK AT IT ANOTHER WAY

Some people try to hide their feelings. Grown-ups sometimes tell you: "Big boys and girls don't cry." If you push your feelings of sadness down inside you, one day they may burst out.

True Stories

I HATE MY BROTHER

My name is Charlene. I'm from a **Caribbean** family. Mom and I used to get along really well. I loved it when she tucked me in at night and told me stories of **Jamaica.** But things have changed. My mom's always yelling at me. It's all my brother Calvin's fault. He messes up my games, so I hit him. Then he goes crying to Mom and she shouts at me.

He messed up my picture!

I wish he'd never been born.

I hate my brother. He gets the attention and all the cuddles. I started shouting at Mum and hiding Calvin's things. Dad said I was being silly. I even dressed like a boy. After all, boys in my family are liked more. But I love my brother even though I hate him. What can I do?

What did you do to him?

I HATE MY BROTHER

Talking It Through

It helps to talk to someone...

AN ADULT

Charlene's Aunt Josie says it is okay to be angry and upset, but it's not okay to hurt Calvin. She suggests that when Charlene gets mad, she goes to her bedroom and punches her pillow.

A COUSIN

Her cousin Wilbert agrees that Calvin can be annoying and gets a lot of the attention because of his age. But he tells Charlene that her family loves her. He says she should tell her mom how she is feeling.

A FRIEND

Her friend Megan says she likes playing with her little sister Lucy. She helps her get dressed and reads her bedtime stories at night. Perhaps Charlene could do the same?

FORWARD STEPS

- **TELL SOMEONE**

  Let a grown-up know when you are upset.

- **EXPRESS YOUR FEELINGS**

  Get rid of your feelings without hurting others.

I decided to tell my mom how I felt. She put me on her lap and said I was still her precious little girl.

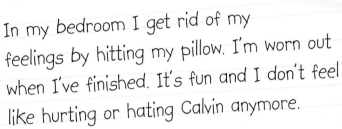

In my bedroom I get rid of my feelings by hitting my pillow. I'm worn out when I've finished. It's fun and I don't feel like hurting or hating Calvin anymore.

Mom said she'd stop Calvin from coming into my room when I'm playing. She set up a star chart for when we play nicely together. I've got loads more stars than Calvin!

At nighttime I go up to listen to Calvin's bedtime story. We both cuddle up to Mom. When Calvin is asleep, Mom braids my hair for school. She says it makes me look really pretty.

True Stories
I MISS MY GRANDMA

I'm Jack. My little brother is named Harry. We get along pretty well, but sometimes we argue. We both agree, though, that our grandma is the greatest. I like going to see her. We sit in her kitchen and she tells us funny stories about when she was little.

Harry and I cried when Mom said Grandma was dying. "It isn't true," I told her angrily.

Now when I visit, Grandma is always in bed. She is thin and can't talk as much. I asked her what would happen when she died. She said, "My body will stop working and the real me will go up to heaven."

Why does she have to die? Why can't she stay here forever?

"What, like a rocket, Grandma?" I asked, remembering the rockets shooting up to the sky in our town's firework display.

"Yes, I think so, Jack," she whispered.

I MISS MY GRANDMA

Talking It Through

It helps to talk to someone...

A PARENT

His dad says he knows how sad Jack is right now. Everyone is, but they have different ways of being sad. He tells Jack to find a special way to remember Grandma after she dies.

AN OLDER FRIEND

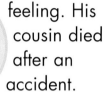

Jack's friend Joe knows how Jack is feeling. His cousin died after an accident. When she was dying, Joe used to sit in the big tree in the park and cry. Crying helped him.

A CLASSMATE

His friend Sophie says she doesn't think it is silly to cry. They can still play together and have lots of fun, but if Jack wants to be sad, she will wait for him until he wants to play again.

FORWARD STEPS

• TALK
Tell someone how you are feeling.

• DO SOMETHING POSITIVE
Find your own special way to say good-bye.

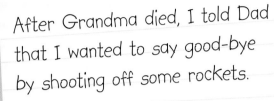

After Grandma died, I told Dad that I wanted to say good-bye by shooting off some rockets.

I took the day off school and went to the **funeral.** I cried when they brought Grandma's box into the chapel. It was covered in flowers.

Then we ate lunch and talked about Grandma. Some people cried and other people laughed. Grandma would have loved to have seen all of her family together.

After dark we went outside. Uncle Bob lit the first rocket. It went w-h-o-o-sh up into the sky. And as each rocket went up, Harry and I shouted: "Bye, Grandma. Bye, Grandma."

I still miss her, but I'm glad I said goodbye in my own special way.

True Stories

A NEW SCHOOL

My name is Maria. My family and I have just moved to a new town. I started a new school today but I don't like it.

I feel really left out. I don't have the right gym clothes and I'm not sure what I should have in my pencil case. It is a big school and I keep getting lost. Worst of all, the girl who my teacher paired me up with just wants to play with her own friends. What am I going to do?

I miss my friends Mark and Katie.

A NEW SCHOOL

Talking It Through

It helps to talk to someone...

A PARENT

Maria's mom gives her a hug and says that Maria will soon make new friends. She promises to take Maria into town over the weekend to get the right gym clothes.

A BIG SISTER

Lauren tells Maria that she has seen some boys and girls her age playing in the park. They are probably from her new school. She offers to take Maria to say hello. Maybe they will let her join in.

A FRIEND

Maria calls Mark. They laugh about his first day at their old school. Mark looked so **lonely!** He has lots of new friends. He says Maria is good at making friends. She will soon be part of the gang.

FORWARD STEPS

- **JOIN IN**
  If you feel lonely, ask to join in.

- **SHARE**
  Find games that you can play together.

I asked Lauren to take me to the park. I was scared, but soon I was playing with two girls from my class.

On Monday I walked to school with Mom. We met my new friends on the way. We chatted so much I think Mom was lonely!

The principal welcomed me to my new school in an assembly and told everyone to remember the Friendship Step in the playground. Children go there if they are looking for someone to play with.

Now my friends and I play hopscotch near the Friendship Step. If there is anyone there, we ask them to join in. My new school helped me feel welcome. Now I welcome other new children.

True Stories

MY BRAINY BEST FRIEND

Hi, I'm Sam. My best friend is named Dipesh.
We're always having fun together. We like
going to each other's house to play. Some
people think we're twins because we're
always doing things together.

When we're at school, I think Dipesh is too
smart. He always wins the prizes. He's the one
who gets a smiley face on his work. Teachers
like him better than me.

It's a shame you have to do extra reading. Soccer would be more fun with you.

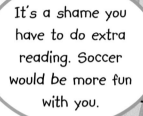

He knows everything. It's not fair!

I get angry because I have to get extra help with my reading. That's when Dipesh gets to learn to play soccer. Then I feel **envious.** I want to be smart like him so I can go outside, too.

If Dipesh wasn't my friend, I wouldn't like him. Sometimes I feel really **jealous.** I get angry with him because I have to work extra hard and he doesn't. I don't like being angry. What can I do?

MY BRAINY BEST FRIEND
Talking It Through

It helps to talk to someone...

A TEACHER

Mrs. Ellis says that everyone has different skills. Sam is good at sports and drawing. She tells Sam that he is great just the way he is and so is Dipesh. That is why they are good friends.

A BIG BROTHER

Jake tells Sam to tell Dipesh how angry he gets and see what Dipesh says. He says that Sam must be smart at some things. He *is* his brother, after all!

A FRIEND

Cheryl says we all have special talents. Sam's talent is making people laugh in class. He is good at sports, too. She says she likes the way he is always smiling.

FORWARD STEPS

- **CHECK IT OUT**
Ask how the other person feels.

- **THINK**
Remember the good things people say about you.

After thinking about it, I told Dipesh I was angry with him for being so brainy. I thought Dipesh would be angry back. But he was upset. He said being smart wasn't that great. Some people think he knows everything. Others call him nerdy and geeky.

He said it doesn't matter if you're smart or dumb. What matters is how good a friend you are and how kind you are.

I don't feel **jealous** of Dipesh anymore. I've got special talents and Dipesh has special talents. And Dipesh teaches me the soccer skills he learns.

From now on I'm going to be proud of Dipesh, my best friend. And I'm going to be proud of myself, too.

Quiz

What Would You Do?

1. What would you do if, like Charlene, you were **jealous** of your brother?
a) Act like a little kid.
b) Be angry with him.
c) Talk to your parents.
d) Complain to your friends.

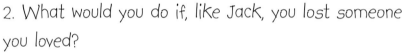

> I wish he'd never been born.

2. What would you do if, like Jack, you lost someone you loved?
a) Get angry and blame others.
b) Cry and find a way to remember the person.
c) Forget all about it.
d) Pretend the person is still here.

3. What would you do if, like Maria, you were **lonely** at your new school?
a) Run away.
b) Hope the problem goes away.
c) Talk your parents into moving back.
d) Make new friends.

4. What would you do if, like Sam, you had a friend who was smarter than you?

a) Say good things about your friend.

b) Say mean things about your friend.

c) Remember things you hate about your friend.

d) Blame your friend for being too brainy.

He knows everything. It's not fair!

Answers

1. c) Instead of letting jealousy eat away at you, tell an adult. Get help finding ways to deal with it.

2. b) Crying helps you to let out the sad feelings you have. When you find your own special way to remember the person, it will help you feel better.

3. d) Running away or ignoring the problem will not help. Making new friends will help ease the sadness of leaving somewhere behind or the fear of moving to a new place.

4. d) If you say good things about yourself and about your friend, you will both be happy.

Glossary

Caribbean   from the eastern and southern West Indies or the Caribbean Sea

confused   feeling mixed-up, not knowing what to do or think

cover-up feeling   feeling that is used to hide how a person is really feeling

emotion   feeling

energy   power a person needs to get things done

envy or envious   feeling of wanting to have things that other people have

funeral   service held a few days after a person dies, often at a church or chapel, to celebrate the person's life

Jamaica   large island country in the Caribbean

jealous or jealousy   feeling of wanting to be like someone else or have something he or she has

loneliness or lonely   being alone and feeling sorry for yourself

new situation   something that a person is going through for the first time

painful loss   losing something or someone very special to you

real feeling   one of four true feelings: anger, fear, joy, or sadness

More Books to Read

Feeney, Kathy. **Feel Good.** Mankato, Minn.: Bridgestone, 2001.

Frost, Helen. **Feeling Angry.** Mankato, Minn.: Capstone, 2000.

Frost, Helen. **Feeling Happy.** Mankato, Minn.: Capstone, 2000.

Frost, Helen. **Feeling Sad.** Mankato, Minn.: Capstone, 2000.

Frost, Helen. **Feeling Scared.** Mankato, Minn.: Capstone, 2000.

Kline, Suzy. **Molly Gets Mad.** New York: Putnam, 2001.

Levete, Sarah. **Being Jealous.** Brookfield, Conn.: Millbrook, 1999.

Schick, Eleanor. **Mama.** Tarrytown, N.Y.: Marshall Cavendish, 2000.

Index